ERNEST C. MANNING

"The Father of Modern Alberta"

A Biographical Sketch

By

TONY CASHMAN
"Edmontonian of the Century"

Cover Sketch of Ernest C. Manning by Garry LaRue

First Authorized by The Alberta Social Credit League
1958
9974 Jasper Avenue, Edmonton, Alberta
Printed in the United States of America

ISBN: 978-1-7371005-7-7

All Scripture quotations are from the King James 1611 Bible.

Republished with permission by
The Old Paths Publications 2021

Address All Inquiries To:
THE OLD PATHS PUBLICATIONS, Inc.
142 Gold Flume Way
Cleveland, Georgia, U.S.A.

Web: www.theoldpathspublications.com
E-mail: TOP@theoldpathspublications.com

Cover sketch of Ernest C. Manning by Garry LaRue

ACKNOWLEDGMENTS

Dr. and Mrs. H. D. Williams of The Old Paths Publications, Inc. prepared the book cover and manuscript for publication. Pastor Jon Harwood and Solid Rock Baptist Church of Calgary paid for the cost of publication. Mr. Frank Crawford re-typed the manuscript and added the Forward, Table of Contents, Notes, About the Author and Addenda. Mr. Ferdinand Gojo scanned the figures and photographs, assisted by Cora Gojo. Mr. Dennis Snyder provided an original copy of the booklet permitting it to be reproduced, thus helping preserve the legacy of Ernest C. Manning and as well, that of William Aberhart, Ernest C. Manning's early mentor and teacher.

FORWARD

Tony Cashman was the Edmonton broadcast journalist for CJCA Radio from 1951 to 1960. He covered the Alberta Legislature during part of E. C. Manning's time as Premier of Alberta. He grew to greatly respect the Premier and was subsequently asked by the Social Credit League in 1958 to produce a biographical portrait of E. C. Manning. This would be the first in depth expose of the man who had already been in power as Premier for fifteen years, and prior to that a Cabinet Minister for eight years during the Aberhart administration. Mr. Cashman considered it a pity that Albertans never got to know the elusive Premier in an up-close-and personal way, because he was so busy with legislative duties and his Bible Institute work. This booklet was published 10 years before the Premier retired from Alberta politics. It was intended to show to the public the character and persona of the man that had led their province to a place of eminence in the Canadian federation and whose administration was considered an economic and moral example for other leaders to follow. Cashman's biography was the first expose of this gifted and private man who many consider to be the most successful and widely respected provincial politician in Canadian history.

Mr. Manning's life was given to serving the citizens of Alberta and Canada over a period of 46 years. He was an Alberta Cabinet Minister for 8 years (1935-1943), Alberta Premier for 25 years (1943-1968) and a Canadian Senator for 13 years (1970-1983). It would be difficult to find anyone who had devoted his whole working life to public service, and at the same time publicly served Jesus Christ preaching the Gospel message.

The work of copying Mr. Cashman's booklet was done in order to preserve E. C. Manning's legacy in Canadian politics during the peak of his career as Premier of the Province of Alberta. Not until 2008 was a comprehensive biography written on Ernest C. Manning by former Calgary Herald reporter, Brian Brennan. His excellent book titled, The Good Steward: The Ernest C. Manning Story, is a must-read for those interested in the Manning-Aberhart years. It was written 40 years after Mr. Manning retired as Alberta's Premier and twelve years after he died in 1996 at the age of 87.

Ernest C. Manning was remarkable in that he came from a farm boy background to become what Mr. Brennan called the Rocky Marciano of Canadian politics, winning seven consecutive elections as Premier of the Province of Alberta. He did this while maintaining a strong fundamentalist Christian testimony, and unashamedly preaching on Canada's National Back to the Bible Hour while leading his province to unparalleled prosperity and success. It is within this consideration of the secular and spiritual needs and well-being of the people under his leadership that Mr. Manning devoted his entire life – and sought no recognition in return. He was indeed "The Good Steward" of Alberta and Albertans as Brian Brennan so aptly named him...and Mr. Cashman so clearly portrayed him in the following pages.

An admirer described the quality of Mr. Cashman's work as an author, journalist and reporter: "he has breathed life into the dusty stuff of history." His Biographical Sketch of E. C. Manning has this quality about it. The Reader is encouraged to follow on and learn about the man called "the Father of modern Alberta" by Ted Byfield, himself called by the Hon. Peter Lougheed, "one of the most knowledgeable observers of Western Canada, and (whose) views are always given significant weight by those involved in public policy decision making." (The Book of Ted, 1998, inside cover)

TABLE OF CONTENTS

SECTION 1

THE IMPORTANCE OF BEING ERNEST

"Who's this fellow Manning, anyway?" That's what Peter Elliott wanted to know in 1948 when the Alberta government hired him to be executive secretary to the Premier. Few people were in a better position to know the answer than Pete. He had been reporting the government beat for the Edmonton Journal for years, and had seen and talked with the Premier almost daily.

However, beyond the facts that Ernest Charles Manning had the best-known face, and the best-known voice in the province; and had been a cabinet minister since 1935, and in 1943 had become the second youngest premier in the history of British parliaments, Pete had no idea what kind of man he was being asked to work for.

That's the problem of E. C. Manning: How can a warm, likeable, straightforward personality, who has been high in the public eye for half of his fifty years, be an unknown?

There are two obvious reasons: At the age of 26 he came directly into the cabinet and into the level of government where a man is sealed off by secretaries. That way, he missed the dozen years at the grassroots when most public figures become known. Secondly, his spare time is so completely taken up with his Bible extension work that he hasn't time for the social life in which most people get acquainted. Those are two obvious reasons, but there is still another, so much more obvious that it has escaped notice. If you, too, have ever wondered: "Who's this fellow Manning?", kindly turn the page.

SECTION 2
THE BEGINNINGS

His parents were English. George Henry Manning was born at Bury St. Edmonds in 1874, but his family were florists and the combination of greenhouses and Bury St. Edmunds was too placid entirely for George Henry. When he was still a lad he attempted to get away from it all in the merchant marine, but his career at sea was cut short when the service found a contradiction between his real age and the age he had put on his application. However, at the turn of the century he was on the sea again, bound for Canada. He was not bound for any particular place in Canada, but most of the young men he fell in with were heading west, so he came to the west too. He came to Winnipeg, worked for a while on a farm near Stonewall, Manitoba, then pushed west again to set up his own farm at Carnduff, Saskatchewan.

With the farm as security he was then able to send for his hometown sweetheart, Elizabeth Dickson. Elizabeth was a frail girl with a tendency to lung trouble, but her doctors advised her to go. English doctors of that time, whose knowledge of western farming came from C.P.R. immigration folders, thought it was great for frail people. Elizabeth came out to Carnduff in 1903 and she and George Manning were married there in the Baptist church.

Their first son William was born in 1905. Ernest was born in 1908, and the next year George Henry Manning made his last move west. He had been hailed out three years in a row and even for the patient little Englishman it was three times and out. The railroad was building a new line southwest from Saskatoon. George decided to get in ahead of the railroad. In the spring of 1909 he filed on a homestead four miles southwest of Rosetown. At the time, Rosetown was strictly a proposed town but George rode the new line as far as it went, rode an ox-drawn wagon twenty miles farther, found the townsite and his homestead. He broke the sod with ox teams and a walking plow, and when Mrs. Manning and the two boys came to the place in the fall, he had the beginnings of a house ready for them.

His farming luck turned for the better right from the filing of the claim. He filed sight unseen, and a neighbor from Carnduff who filed the same day in the Saskatoon land office happened to pick a quarter section of knobby sandhills that resisted every effort to make a farm out of them. But George Manning landed on rich black gumbo that produced rich, golden wheat; and with luck and good farming he managed comfortably well. He was able to buy another quarter section, and lease a half section and eventually had 640 acres to his farm.

Roy, the third and last of the young Mannings, was born there. In time, all three boys were going to the Glenpayne School, half a mile away. The school's one room was up and closed some years ago, but the initials of the Manning boys are still carved on the desks. Roy, who runs the old family farm; Bill, a high school teacher and city councilor in Saskatoon; and Ernest, of whom people ask: "Who's this fellow Manning, anyway?"

The farm life was hard, but the Mannings were English and the English serenity and sense of humor, which was equal to two world wars, was equal to homesteading in Saskatchewan. The boys were assigned their responsibilities on the farm, and as they became teenagers had to take turns managing the entire operation. Still, with all the work, the Mannings had fun and most of it was sparked by Ernest.

Ernest was a natural entertainer. He played the fiddle in the local dance band, and his teacher thought he might have become very good at the violin if he hadn't been interested in so many other things. The other things were mechanical. In the heyday of "Popular Mechanics" magazine there was no reader more avid than E. C. Manning of Rosetown. It was he who talked his conservative father into converting the farm from horsepower to machinery, and having talked the elder Manning into it, he then had to figure out how the things worked, and – even more important – how to get them working again when they quit. If there's one man E. C. Manning envies today it's probably Wetaskiwin implement dealer Stan Reynolds, for his collection of antique tractors. When he tours a new hospital, the Premier is likely to spend most of the time in the boiler room, peering at the gauges and asking how they work.

The prize mechanical possession of his youth was a model T Ford which he christened "The Bazoo," and later paid twenty-five dollars for another one – taking parts off it to keep the first one going. In company with teenagers all over the continent he advanced the cam gear of his jalopy a couple of notches to encourage it to greater speeds than Mr. Ford had dreamed of. Just how fast "The Bazoo" would go the Premier cannot tell exactly, because, in addition to having no windshield, no headlights and no muffler, the car had no speedometer. However, he guesses that the top speed was about sixty miles an hour on a good road. Rocketing down the trail to Rosetown, Ernest added his bit to the significance of the expression: the roaring twenties. He liked to sweep into town at full speed and pull in behind the smartest new coupe on the main street.

One night as he drove the hired man home from town Ernest heard the man shouting with fear. This was great sport, thought our hero: he would give the poor man an even faster ride, and did. Just in time he discovered why the poor fellow was shouting. He had been sitting with his feet dangling from the back and his trousers had caught fire. Ernest braked the contraption to a cylinder-popping halt, and rolled the man in the ditch.

One time, in the spirit of fun, he swung his gentle little mother to the top of a cupboard, from which she could not get down. Another time he hugged her so hard he cracked two of her ribs. But her English sense of humor was equal even to the exuberance of E. C. Manning, teen-ager.

Mr. Diefenbaker has a good story about being caught out in a winter storm in Saskatchewan; Mr. Manning has a good one about a storm in summer. He and his father were out driving in "The Bazoo" when they sensed that a storm was coming. It had been a hot, still day, and darkness came early as the western sky built up a wall of black cloud higher than Everest. The stillness became a dead, foreboding calm. Even the birds disappeared, as though taking cover. The Mannings could hear the wind before it struck, but they couldn't go fast enough to get home ahead of it. The featherweight car was pushed off the road as the hurricane swept over it. Father and son dove for the ditch, and lay there all night as the storm cracked and shrieked above them like an artillery barrage. In the vivid green flashes that preceded the thunder they could see the whole countryside writhing in torment. At dawn, when the storm had passed on, they drove home with caution, picking their way through the debris.

On the Manning farm, as on every western farm of that day, some of the most popular reading was the small order catalogue. Simpson's; Montgomery-Ward; Sears-Roebuck; those were the names that held as much glamor as Clara Bow; Mary Pickford; Douglas Fairbanks. Ernest liked to read about all the fascinating mechanical things that could be ordered by mail. In the fall of 1924, having prospered to the extent of a hundred dollars or so on harvest work, he decided to invest it in the most fascinating item in all the catalogues: a three-tube radio offered by Sears-Roebuck of Chicago for $103.00. The radio came complete with a gooseneck loudspeaker, and earphones for listening to distant stations. Ernest sent the money, but Sears-Roebuck, it appeared, did not send the radio. Weeks went by, months went by, and no radio. Ernest decided sadly that he had placed too much confidence in Sears-Roebuck and that his money was gone. Then, just before Christmas, there was a card from the postmaster in Rosetown. He was holding the radio for customs duty – something the consignee hadn't thought of – and would the consignee please come get it, or it would have to be sold. Ernest brought the radio out to the farm on Christmas eve, and on Christmas day, 1924, while the wind blew cold and gray out of the northwest, Ernest and his brother Roy clambered to the roof and set up the aerial.

The radio changed all their lives. That winter, the Mannings lived for cold, clear nights, when distant stars would be visible in the clear air, and distant radio signals would come through the radio. The radio affected all their lives, but the most profound effect was on Ernest. One Sunday afternoon in the fall of 1925 he picked up CFCN in Calgary, and heard William Aberhart broadcasting from the Palace Theatre. Every Sunday at three, Ernest would be listening to Aberhart.

SECTION 3
CALGARY

The Mannings were a solidly religious family in the Baptist tradition, and attended the United Church in Rosetown. But they were not more noticeably religious than other families where a blessing is invoked on dinner. The Manning boys were very intense in their interests and when Ernest became interested in Aberhart's Bible broadcasts it was natural that his interest would become intense. Of course, many youngsters like that get tired of things quickly and go intently from one thing to another – and Mrs. Manning was grateful that some of the hobbies didn't last very long – but the second son's interest in Aberhart's teaching grew more intense with each Sunday broadcast.

Mr. Aberhart was a Fundamental Baptist. In the late nineteenth century "the higher criticism" had moved through the Baptist Church, starting in Germany. The higher criticism maintained that the Bible contains the word of God but no one could say for sure how much or what verses. Then, after the higher critics had put the Bible in its place, the Fundamentalists came along to put the higher critics in their place. Mr. Aberhart was a Fundamentalist, a down-to-earth Fundamentalist, a down-to-bedrock Fundamentalist. In fact, Mr. Aberhart was right down to the *D3 on this, as he was in all his convictions. The Bible was ALL the Word of God, every syllable; and if everything in it was the Word of God, then the prophecies must also be inspired. And since not all the prophecies were fulfilled in the New Testament, and in fact many more prophecies were added, then the prophecies must be moving toward fulfillment in the events of the day.

* The Upper Devonian D3 contains the Leduc reef complex where oil was discovered in 1947 setting off Alberta's enduring 'oil boom,' and the prosperity that followed. It was found at a drilling depth of 5300 to 6100 feet in the Edmonton area.

This fascinated the young Saskatchewan farm boy. Mr. Aberhart was a gifted, illuminating teacher, and he made the same impression on young Manning, listening on the radio, that he did teaching Mathematics and English to his kids at Crescent Heights High School in Calgary. Alberta's eighth premier says he became a Christian listening to Aberhart – that he became convinced it was not enough to know ABOUT Christ – but that he wanted to know Christ personally.

So, in the fall of 1926, when the harvest was complete, young Manning decided that he would not invest his money in the mail-order catalogue but he would go to Calgary for a holiday and meet Aberhart. He took the train. There is a popular legend that he hitch-hiked, but that form of travel was impractical in 1926 and he was a very practical youth. He stayed at the Y.M.C.A. in Calgary, introduced himself to Aberhart, and looked in on the young people's group at Westbourne Baptist Church, where Aberhart was on the board of deacons. We chose the term "looked-in" with care, because that's about all he did on his first visit to Calgary.

There were 200 young people in the group, and in among them was Muriel Preston, three years younger than Ernest, who would spend part of every evening at the piano. Muriel came by music honestly. Her father, William Preston, had come from England to be cantorist tenor with the famous Trinity Church Choir of New York.

Later he had sung in churches in Winnipeg, Toronto and Saskatoon, and he died in Saskatoon when Muriel was five years old. Muriel spent some years in convent schools in Prince Albert and Calgary, and got her first formal training in music from the nuns. When Ernest saw her for the first time she was studying with Annie Glen Broder, the Calgary music pioneer, who was as colorful as any pioneer in any line to operate in Calgary. Muriel's mother, Mrs. Mary Preston, was teaching at Center School, and was associated with Mr. Aberhart in many of his projects. The young man from Saskatchewan knew very little of this, and wouldn't have cared much if he had. He and Muriel made little impression on each other; but of course, many things can change in ten years.

* Above note added by Frank Crawford.

SECTION 4

THE PROPHETIC BIBLE INSTITUTE

Through the Sundays of the winter of 1926-27 he heard Aberhart describe the process of his plans to build a Prophetic Bible Institute, a school to teach prophetic study of the Scriptures, which would be open to young people, and which would, in effect, be a sort of junior college. He needed $65,000 to build it, and had all kinds of schemes to raise the money – at one time he had his Sunday school selling bricks for a quarter. Young Manning heard him announce the success of the fund-raising, that construction was starting, on Eighth Avenue East, and that it would be opening in the fall. He decided that he would be a student in the first class, and when the Institute opened in October, he was there, along with 35 other youngsters.

He literally worked his way through college. The courses were arranged to run from October to April, so farm youngsters could take advantage of them. Half the students came in from the country. Young Manning operated his father's farm, and he and his brothers did custom harvesting for the neighbors.

In his second and third years he lived with the Aberharts. Mr. Aberhart had two daughters but he had never had a son, and Ernest came close to filling the bill. Mr. Aberhart helped him round out his secondary education, which had become a bit disorganized in the schools of rural Saskatchewan, and Mrs. Aberhart did her best to add some substance to his frame – which was as lean as his stripped-down model T. The author of this biography has feasted on "Heavenly Hash," one of Mrs. Aberhart's favorite frozen desserts – a thing compounded of three-quarters of a pound of graham wafers, three-quarters of a pound of miniature marshmallows, a half-pound of maraschino cherries, two cups of walnuts, one can of Eagle Brand condensed milk, and a top sprinkling of icing sugar – and it is well named. Things like "Heavenly Hash" did wonders for Mr. Aberhart but they didn't add a pound to his prize student.

In his last year as a student, Ernest was also on the teaching staff of the Institute. Mr. Aberhart, after a day teaching at Crescent Heights, would come in and teach night classes, and on Sundays he would broadcast. At one time he was on the air almost five hours every Sunday, over CFCN. From ten to eleven there was a "morning broadcast," aimed particularly at the children. From eleven to twelve-fifteen there was a service from the Bible Institute Baptist Church. Then from three to five there was the Prophetic Bible Conference, which first caught the attention of E. C. Manning. Then from six to six-thirty Mr. Aberhart was on again with an evening hymn program. In 1930, when Mr. Aberhart went to the coast for his annual holiday, he asked the 21-year-old Manning to take over his radio work, and from that time on they shared the work.

Muriel Preston by this time was the permanent organist and pianist for the Institute. In 1933 she went on a tour of Alberta with the American evangelist Charles Neighbor. It was Mr. Neighbor who originated the slogan "Back to the Bible," a slogan that became very important in the Manning career later on. Mr. Neighbor's tour was arranged by Aberhart as an extension of the Institute work. They spent a week at a time at Edmonton, Wetaskiwin, Stettler, Claresholm and Lethbridge – and at Lethbridge, Gerry Gaetz came down early Sunday morning and put CJOC on the air so Mr. Neighbor could broadcast.

William Aberhart's interest in young people was legendary, and the legend was well earned. It's unfortunate that people who knew him only as an embattled politician, with dissention in his party, and the bondholders banging on the door, could never have seen him officiating at a kid's ball game, or organizing the games at a young people's picnic. Full of Wagnerian good spirits, Aberhart was the center of the fun. The students at Crescent Heights lost track of the number of student "companies" Mr. Aberhart incorporated. A typical student corporation was the one he organized to buy a movie projector for the school. The kids bought in at ten cents a share. That was Aberhart as not enough people knew him. His brilliant mind made a game of mathematics, and applied the science of mathematics to life. After working out a problem in geometry he would digress to tell his class that life was a science like mathematics with a rigid set of values. "You must have a standard of values in life," he would intone; "and you must never get your values mixed up."

It was this interest in young people that led William Aberhart into a project bigger than anything he had ever organized before. The depression was grinding deeper into the life of the country, eroding the economy and eroding the spirit of the people, especially the young people. Aberhart would meet his most brilliant graduates. He would ask them how they were getting along and they would tell him they weren't getting along very well – they couldn't get jobs.

This bothered Aberhart. How the dickens, he wondered, can we be in the midst of all this plenty, with all these resources to be developed, and yet have no work for my most brilliant students? To Aberhart, the mathematician, these things just didn't add up. The director of the Prophetic Bible Institute was not the man to keep his thoughts to himself. He would pose this question to anyone in hearing distance. In the spring of 1932, when he came to Edmonton to mark examination papers, he put it at lunch one day to C. M. Scarborough, a teacher at Victoria High School. Mr. Scarborough asked him if he had read "Economic Nationalism" by Maurice Colbourne. Aberhart recognized the name. Maurice Colbourne was an English actor who had toured western Canada in more prosperous times. He was surprised to hear that Colbourne had written a book on economics; he asked Mr. Scarborough was it was about. His companion told him it outlined the Douglas theory of Social Credit.

SECTION 5
SOCIAL CREDIT

Aberhart had never heard of the book, but within two days he had read it, and in a very short time he had read everything he could get hold of on the subject of Social Credit, and was in lively correspondence with Major Douglas. He and his 23-year-old Institute manager spent many evenings that summer discussing the theory. As Major Douglas saw the problem, there was unemployment because there wasn't enough purchasing power in the hands of the people to buy what the people could produce. If the purchasing power could be increased to equal productive power there would be work for everybody. To Aberhart, the mathematician, it worked out like a simple equation.

In Regina about the same time, the C.C.F. party emerged with the *"planned economy" as a cure for unemployment. Mr. Aberhart, with all his organizing talent could not see himself organizing the entire economy, and he could see no need for anything so drastic. There was nothing basically wrong with the economy. It just needed more purchasing power to make it work. He became convinced that the "money barons," who controlled the flow of money, were keeping money out of the hands of the people. He began talking about Social Credit in his Sunday broadcasts.

> * The provincial government would 'control' the economy becoming involved in planning, managing, production and marketing for certain key sectors of the economy and social welfare as well. It would be socialism versus free democracy – collectivism versus individualistic free enterprise. Aberhart and Manning

were both anti-socialism but not anti-social justice in a free enterprise context.

What happened after that happened so swiftly that even Mr. Aberhart was left breathless. But it's the way things happen in the Alberta climate when conditions are right. When cold winter air lies thick and motionless on the southern foothills a chinook can pour down from the mountains and churn it away in an hour. In northern Alberta in summer, when the lakes lie still in the suffocating afternoon calm, they build up sudden, crashing storms overhead. Conditions were right in the depressed summer of 1935.

When the storm broke William Aberhart was swept into the Premier's office, and Ernest C. Manning was swept in alongside him. Manning headed the polls in Calgary. On September 3rd, he became the second youngest minister in the history of British parliaments. Only Pitt the Younger was younger when he became Chancellor of the Exchequer in 1782. Pitt was 23; Manning was still short of 27.

The next April he and Muriel Preston were married at the Bible Institute church. Reverend Roy Taylor, M.L.A. from Coleman, performed the ceremony. And giving the bride away, one vast substantial smile like Mrs. Fezziwig, was William Aberhart.

* Above note added by Frank Crawford.

THE MANNINGS AT HOME, 1916

Seventeen

ERNEST   WILLIAM   AND   ROY

THE MANNINGS AT HOME, 1952

PRESTON AND KEITH

25

TO THE
HONOURABLE
ERNEST CHARLES
MANNING
·PREMIER·OF·ALBERTA·

Honourable Sir:

Upon the occasion of your Fiftieth Birthday, your fellow Citizens of the Province of Alberta desire to convey to you their most sincere congratulations.... We are reminded at this time that since 1935, when you became the youngest Minister of the Crown in the Commonwealth, you have devoted Twenty-Three continuous years ... almost half your lifetime ... to the Service of our Province and our People. During those years you have displayed, by precept and by example, the most capable leadership. In the period of your Ministry our Province has grown in Stature, our People have Prospered, and have enjoyed an ever growing measure of Economic Democracy and Social Justice.

In token of our Esteem this Address is presented to you, Honourable Sir, with the Prayer that God will spare you many more fruitful years in which to serve our Queen, our Province and our People.

Dated at Edmonton, in the Province of Alberta, September 20, 1958.

W HORBAY

A

MANNING SHOWS HIS CAR TO
ADMIRING COUSIN, GRACE DIXON

Eighteen

MANNING SHOWS HIS CATCH TO
ADMIRING HOST, MAJOR JIM LOWERY

Nineteen

SECTION 6

THE MONTHS THAT MADE MANNING

Some men have greatness thrust upon them, but not all of them are able to handle it. Ernest C. Manning had it thrust upon him by the Social Credit sweep, but he held it fast, and in the eighteen months from September 1935 to February 1937 secured his present position. The opportunity was great, but he was equal to it.

The new government had so many troubles that Job would likely have thought twice about changing places with Aberhart. The new government had been accepted by the majority in 55 of Alberta's 63 ridings, but it had no acceptance whatever in business and financial circles. To the youngest minister, in the new ministry of Trade and Industry, went the task of being ambassador to this group, many of whose members thought the dark ages had returned.

Manning was invited to speak everywhere: to chambers of commerce, boards of trade, industrial conferences, service clubs and university clubs. At some of these affairs he must have felt like a Christian of an earlier age waiting to meet the lions. He was pitted against some of the sharpest minds in the province, among people who hadn't taken Social Credit very seriously before the election, and were now determined to find out what it was, and what manner of men had a five-year contract to install it.

He was 27, and with his slight build and his glasses and pale, studious face he looked younger. But he made a favorable impression; neither aggressive nor defensive, speaking calmly and clearly so his listeners got the idea even if they couldn't agree with it. He enhanced this favorable impression answering questions. They were questions that could not merely be answered but had to be met head-on. And he developed a technique which he uses today when receiving a delegation. Many questions were loaded – some carried an extra load of sarcasm or derision – but no matter how trying the questioner Manning would hear him out, listening with complete, searching attention – an attention disarming and disconcerting. Then, without a visible trace of anger, temper or ill-feeling he would produce a calm, lucid answer. We doubt that he made a single convert in these personal appearances but he made Social Credit respectable and himself respected.

As minister of Trade and Industry he was also drawn into labor-management disputes as moderator. And here he had to overcome more personal difficulties. Although he was well-versed in labor and management on farms, he had no experience in city labor, and his only business experience had been managing the Bible Institute. However, his fairness and ability to analyze a problem in clear terms made another good impression.

Then there was life in the Legislature. Those were days of confusion, when 55 men who had never sat there before were learning to run the government, and many of them were determined to be better Social Creditors than the Premier. Mr. Aberhart, for all his talents, had no talent for parliament. This was put down to his having been a teacher. Perhaps if Mr. Aberhart had had the good fortune to teach under the "enterprise" system he might have been better at the give-and-take of parliament, but he was a teacher in the old school, whose word was the last word. In the confusion Manning emerged as the floor leader of the party. Cool, calm, fair in debate, willing to listen but always in control – in the opposition cloakrooms you heard nothing but good about Manning.

In all this there was only one flaw for the newlywed Mrs. Manning. The man who talked so fluently to chambers of commerce, mediation boards and sittings of the Legislature, seemed to run completely out of conversation when he got into his own house. The new Mrs. Manning took it up with her mother-in-law when she came to visit. And she said: "I know, dear. I could never get his father to talk, but now that I'm old and deaf and can't hear him anyway he talks all the time. You'll come to it."

The grind continued. It was a grind that could have broken the young man politically and almost broke him physically. In November, 1936, his doctors discovered he had tuberculosis. He was told that complete rest was the only cure, so he went to bed in his home in the Garneau district and stayed there with the same determination that he attacked every other problem. He made a remarkable recovery, and when he was welcomed back into the Legislature on February 23, 1937, it was clear that the party was welcoming its next leader.

SECTION 7

MR. PREMIER

He tried to join the army when war broke out in 1939, but the army doctors found the scars on his lung, and they also discovered a heart valve that didn't come up to army standards. However, he talked himself into the militia, and was assigned to the 49th Battalion as Lieutenant Manning, C.E. He drilled twice a week, went on week-end exercises, went to Sarcee for summer training and had reached the rank of Captain when the pressure of being Premier forced him to give it up.

Aberhart grew weaker and weaker during the session of 1943. Meeting Alf Hooke in the hall one day he said, "I don't know how a man can feel so weak and still live." He went to the coast after the session but his strength did not return and he died there.

There was no doubt about his successor. Manning, at 34, was the youngest man in the government, in fact the youngest in the Legislature. Solon Low, the party's leading writer, wanted the leadership, but the older men voted for Manning in a meeting that took less than an hour on June 3rd, 1943. He was again second only to Pitt, who became a first minister at the age of 24. At the beginning he sought the advice of the older men in the cabinet – particularly Dr. Cross and Mr. Fallow – but the final decision would be his, and the older men went along with his judgment.

Almost immediately he began to move out from under the shadow of Aberhart. You may have read that Manning spoke with the voice of Aberhart, but that's not quite accurate. If it was Manning broadcasting from the

Bible Institute you might say: "Is that Manning; or, is it Aberhart?" But if it was Aberhart; well, it was Aberhart.

Many writers have noted the similarity in the voice and have suggested that the only difference between the men was in size. It's true that at 250 pounds Mr. Aberhart was almost twice the man his successor was, but these "weigh-in" figures are but one indication of the basic differences. Aberhart weighed 250 pounds because he was of German descent, with a heavy German build and a Wagnerian appetite. Manning weighed about half that because he is of English descent, with a spare English frame, and an admirable restraint about food.

The ethnic differences are apparent in all their actions.

Aberhart loved a fight: Manning prefers peace but will not back away from a fight.

Aberhart shook his fist; Manning has put his hands behind his back and squeezed the knuckles white rather than lose his temper.

Aberhart was a talker; Manning is a listener. He has made a great asset of his powers as a listener, and tells his sons Keith and Preston: "You can't learn anything when you're talking."

Aberhart thought there was one side to an argument. If you're arguing one side of a question, Manning will argue the other side even if he agrees with you.

Aberhart was dogmatic; Manning is diplomatic.

Aberhart said "I'm going," and he was gone; Manning says, "I'd like to get there," and usually does.

Aberhart instilled either love or hate in people: Manning instills confidence.

Aberhart won friends and influenced people by his fire; Manning does it with cool perception. Manning's judgment is better than Aberhart's, except perhaps in the matter of judging people. His close associates say he doesn't suspect people of being what they CAN be.

Manning is the better administrator; but it's doubtful whether an older Manning could make such a political breakthrough as Aberhart did in 1935.

On another point, there is no doubt whatever: Aberhart could not delegate authority; Manning can. In fact, people who try to bypass his ministers are told firmly what the ministers are for. His ministers say they run their departments without interference, and feel free to discuss things in public which are not yet government policy. And although they enjoy his non-interference they seek his advice, for the penetrating analysis he can give. One minister says: "He's got one of the most analytical minds in the province. He's got to see the end from the beginning." Another veteran cabineteer told about a brief he and his staff worked out, a brief with forty recommendations. For days, they asked each other every question they could, and thought they had all the answers. The Premier looked it over, and said: "I agree with 38 of the sections, but if you do this, the end result will be so-and-so. If you do that, the end result will be such-and-such."

He has a phenomenal capacity for details, and can seldom get his fill of detailed information on a subject at hand. When he goes to buy a car, he wants to know everything about it. What is the wheelbase? What is the displacement of the pistons? In what order to the cylinders fire? What is the compression ratio? A salesman hoping to sell the Premier a car has to know more about it than the designer. His detailed knowledge of government has benefitted from experience in no less than five ministries: Provincial Secretary, Trade and Industry, Provincial Treasurer, Mines and Minerals, and Attorney General.

He has few pet expressions but he's been often heard to say: "That fellow always goes off at half-cock." Manning seldom does, if ever. Before he talks he knows what he's going to say, and has also figured out what other people will say about what he's going to say. When he speaks publicly he talks from notes that are really individual words. One page of apparently disconnected words will represent an hour's speech in the Legislature. But the words are carefully chosen, no matter what the occasion. Make this test. In any official function, when a string of dreary, rambling speeches followed the dinner, see who makes the only clear, coherent and connected speech?

Manning the Premier, like any other real leader, has private thoughts on which no one intrudes, and not even men who have been with him in government since the beginning call him Ernie – he gets Ernie only from his brothers. He can keep his real thoughts so well concealed that it has taken many years for his colleagues to discover the signs that he is steaming inside. The muscles around his mouth will tighten and he will say:

"Well now, I don't think I would have done it just that way."

The deft, probing thinker is usually a man with a sense of humor, and Manning is no exception. There was a time, for example, when he followed D. M. Duggan in the budget debate. Mr. Duggan had been a Conservative leader in the house, but switched to the Independent label in 1940. He was the opposition budget critic, and used to tell the government how much money it could save if it would listen to him. The year Mr. Duggan returned as an Independent, he suggested economies which would have saved only half as much as the year before. Manning observed that Mr. Duggan was probably less Conservative now.

Then there was the time a health bill was under discussion. Dr. Morrish spoke, then Dr. McPherson spoke, then Dr. Cross spoke, then Ed Fee, the undertaker, spoke. Manning said that was appropriate because Mr. Fee had been following the medical profession for a long time.

Then there was the time the cabinet was discussing what to give an important visitor to the province. The visitor was a lady and happened to be single. Manning thought they might give her Gordon Taylor, Alberta's bachelor Minister of Highways.

SECTION 8
BACK TO THE BIBLE

But is he sincere? That question bothers so many people because people are funny. If a man in public life says he is trying to follow the teachings of Kant or Ghandi or Bernarr McFadden or Machiavelli or Dorothy Dix or William the Conqueror, people merely say: "Isn't that interesting?" But if he says he is trying to follow the teachings of God people say, "Is he sincere?"

Well, all right, assuming he's sincere about that, is he sincere about his Bible broadcasting?

The best answer to both these questions is probably the fact that he left home at the age of nineteen to make prophetic Bible teaching his life work. That was in 1927, long before anyone but Major Douglas had thought about Social Credit. In the years that J. J. Bowlen sat in the Legislature no one ever asked him if he was sincere about ranching. Do you suppose that Mr. Prowse is sincere about law; or that Mr. Hawrelak is sincere about Orange Crush?

In the early days he liked to have hecklers question him about mixing religion with politics. He would answer without anger that religion is something that should not be taken down from the shelf on Sundays. He would go on to say that you can't divorce spiritual values from the things of everyday life. He would say that a right relationship with God must precede a right relationship with man. And the hecklers would retire in confusion.

There's a point that should be noted about his Bible broadcasting. While he insists that religion cannot be kept out of politics, he keeps politics out of religion. Mr. Aberhart began preaching social justice and wound up preaching Social Credit; Manning does not go beyond social justice.

If he were haled into court – by his own Attorney General's department – and asked to prove his sincerity, he might have a job because sincerity is an intangible. However, he would have no trouble at all proving his consistency. His pattern of Bible extension work has not varied since 1930 when he began sharing broadcasts with Aberhart.

When he came to Edmonton in 1935 they added a Sunday night broadcast from the Capitol Theatre. One Sunday Aberhart would be in Calgary for the afternoon broadcast and Manning would be in Edmonton for the evening program. The next Sunday they would trade. As if that weren't enough week-end activity Manning also accepted a request to take a Bible class for a Baptist group which held Sunday meetings at the Orange Hall on 114th Street. He created such interest in this group that the group got too large for the Orange Hall and moved to the Masonic Temple. When the Sunday night broadcasting was abandoned, he started a shorter Sunday morning program on CFRN: "Christian Reveille." As a sideline to this program he organized another adult study group, the Christian Laymen's Forum, and continued as director of the Masonic Temple classes. This group became so large and established that it gradually became a congregation, and in 1948 the members decided to build their own Fundamental Baptist Church – at Jasper and 118th Street. They called a permanent pastor then, and Manning was able to withdraw from active direction – and take on the biggest Bible extension project of his career.

Back in Calgary the Prophetic Bible Institute was having trouble keeping its broadcast on the air at the historic time of three o'clock Sunday afternoon. The directors asked the Premier for help. He felt it was his responsibility, and he and Mrs. Manning began travelling to Calgary every week-end.

On winter week-ends when other people were glad to stay close to home the Mannings drove to Calgary. On summer week-ends when other people drove to the lake the Mannings drove to Calgary. During the week he would arrange the program and she would arrange the music. The musicians included violinist Mary Short, the concertmaster with the Calgary Symphony Orchestra. In October, 1948, they extended the broadcast to Edmonton through CFRN. Two months later they added Vancouver and Regina. And in September, 1949, when the program was extended to Grande Prairie, Vernon and Victoria, they adopted the name "Back to the Bible Hour." Early in 1950, with an encouraging mail response from the Winnipeg area, a Winnipeg station was added to the chain. In August it reached into Ontario, through Barrie, and in September it went coast to coast, with the addition of Ottawa, Sarnia and Halifax. And in December, 1951, Hamilton and Saskatoon came onto the tape-recorded network. In 1953, the Mannings made a national tour, holding meetings in most of these places, and were more than surprised by the large crowds. Three years ago, the pressure of commuting to Calgary every week-end became too great, and the musicians now commute to Edmonton instead, which makes the enterprise even more expensive.

It costs fifty to sixty thousand dollars a year to keep the series on the air and it all comes in freewill donations from listeners. Well, almost all of it – if there's a deficit the Premier has to take care of it. The programs go on every Sunday of the year, and when the Mannings want to get away for a holiday they are recorded in advance. While driving through New York State not long ago they heard their own program on the car radio, coming from Halifax.

The founder of the "Back to the Bible Hour" thinks of it as twentieth century evangelism. It has the same objective and the same message as the old-time evangelism but the presentation is geared to the twentieth century and takes advantage of the progress in this century. The old-time revivalist had to shout because he didn't have the radio. E. C. Manning is grateful for the improvements, because he isn't much given to shouting, and because the radio can carry the Gospel to a wider audience than the nineteenth century preacher ever dreamed of. Even if a man won't leave his house to hear a sermon the radio will take it right to him, and even if the man is listening for the sake of argument, the preacher can still deliver his message. He finds radio ideal for spreading prophetic study of the Bible, because radio aims at the majority audience, and most people are interested in current events, and the "Back to the Bible Hour" holds this interest by relating the historic and prophetic message of the Bible to what's going on today.

Radio itself has changed since E. C. Manning sent away to Sears-Roebuck for his first set. Mr. Aberhart used to talk on for two hours then. In maintaining the Aberhart tradition his successor offers a skillfully-paced thirty-minute production which keeps the accelerated pace of today's radio. The veteran Edmonton theatre man, Walter Wilson, says he never had a man on the Capitol Theatre stage with a better sense of timing than the director of the "Back to the Bible Hour."

The national success of the program has made more work for two of the director's hardest working, unpaid assistants. They are Charles Pearce, the chairman of the provincial marketing board, and his wife. The Pearces do printing for a hobby, and in the basement of their home on University Avenue they have what appears to be a complete printing shop. The program offers a Sunday school by correspondence, and every week the Pearces print and mail Sunday school lessons to 45 hundred kids, including 400 in the new dominion of Ghana. They also print tracts and pamphlets by the rack full, and put out The Prophetic Voice, a monthly magazine with a circulation of 44 hundred. The magazine is a digest of current writing on prophetic study and is sent to supporters of the broadcast. The Pearces edit it, cut it, stitch it and mail it. Every year now they put out 750 thousand pieces of literature in what they describe as "Mr. Manning's work."

Mr. Manning's work will go on, and it should be made clear that his plans do not include starting a new church. He is firmly content with the tenets of the Fundamental Baptist Church, and will go on trying to show people of any church – or no church – that the Bible offers a guide to life – the present life and the one after – and that study of the prophecies is a fascinating intellectual pursuit. Here, perhaps is a clue to his approach to the work: Among the people in the Bible he has a particular fondness for the Apostle Paul.

SECTION 9

WHO'S THIS FELLOW MANNING?

The magazines gave up on E. C. Manning years ago. Their writers used to concoct some rich, heady prose for him – stuff like "the pole-thin Premier who sells oil with the Bible in one hand…" Another writer created this weird apparition: "the pale Premier with the pale eyes." But he is not really pale; his complexion is sandy and healthy, and his eyes are not pale either; they are a substantial blue. That kind of prose is beloved to editors but it gives the reader little light on the subject: "Who's this fellow Manning anyway?"

The fellow lives on a farm seven miles and twenty minutes northeast of the city. The farm is bounded on the east and south by the Saskatchewan River – which takes ten acres off the regulation 320 for the service. It's a well-appointed dairy farm, which ships milk from a herd of thirty Holsteins, and there are also a few Shorthorns for experiments in raising beef cattle. In these surroundings, in a handsome ranch-style house, the fellow lives a cheerful family life with Muriel and their two boys – Keith, born in 1940, and Preston, who arrived in 1942. Keith has had to contend with cerebral palsy all his life but has tackled the problem with characteristic Manning determination. He likes farming and hopes to buy out his father eventually. Preston inherits his father's mechanical bent. After Preston and his friends spent some months assembling a car with parts gleaned from the Beverly dump, the Mannings decided it would be safer to buy him a new car. Keith and Preston call their father "Pop," and kid him about his "Sunday walk" – the series of stiff strides with which he comes out on the stage for a "Back to the Bible Hour" broadcast.

The Premier's greatest regret of recent years was that he could not see more of his own father, who died in 1956, at the age of 82. The old gentleman was always being urged to come for visits, but he was too busy. He was needed at the hospital in Rosetown. The Premier's mother had spent a year in the hospital before she died in 1949. The old gentleman had gone to see her every day, and when she died he still came every day. (He thought the local barber was charging the patients too much for shaves and used to bring a shaving outfit and trim them for nothing.) He followed his son's progress with interest in the newspapers and his entertaining letters would often begin: "Dear Ernie: What the dickens have you been saying now?" He would explain again, in closing, that he was too busy to come for a visit.

The favorite relaxation of his son, who is also a busy man, is getting out on the farm tractor. Or, if there is no reasonable excuse for the tractor, shingling a barn will do. His interest in farming was pointed up when the Public Works Department took advantage of his absence to refurnish his office in the Legislative Building. They cleaned out everything, including two walls of pictures which had been accumulating since Mr. Rutherford's time. When the Premier returned he sat down at his new desk – in his new chair – swiveled around, and said: "Uh huh! Uh huh!" and then asked: "Where's my bull?" The bull was named Killearn Max William – it was a Shorthorn which Claude Gallinger had sold for $15,000 – not to the Premier but to someone else. However, he had given the Premier a framed picture of Killearn Max William, and of all the hundred pictures that had been carted out of the office that was the one he wanted back.

The farm is remote enough for any man, and the one road to it is patrolled by gravel trucks which race back and forth to a gravel pit, discouraging all but the most intrepid. However, many letters come to the farm from people who have heard the "Back to the Bible Hour," and want personal advice. And the place is connected to the cares of civilization by telephone. Muriel can entertain her husband and sons with first-rate impersonations of the inebriates who phone the Premier and want to tell him off. Neither she nor her husband drink or smoke. He had a smoke once when he was made an Indian Chief by the Blood Indians and had to smoke the peace pipe – but this experience did not cause him to add smoking to his interests.

He also likes to cook – grilled charcoal steaks – but that is his one culinary achievement and his interest in food is not great. Although he is not pole-thin, he is a light eater and his waistline and hairline have held their positions through the years.

He also finds relaxation in his hi-fi set, drawing the line only at opera, and when his record collection doesn't provide just what he wants he will get out his fiddle and beat out some old-time stuff, echoes of cheerful nights around Rosetown.

When he reads for relaxation he likes mystery stories, but his favorite reading is about yachting. He probably has more books about yachts and ships than any man in Edmonton. He likes the sea in all its moods and when he's on vacation near the ocean he will sit on a deck chair just watching. On days when the sea is too sullen and mean for other people, it still fascinates E. C. Manning. To his regret, he has been able to get away for a sea voyage only once. That was in 1952 when he and Mrs. Manning went to the Coronation. They also visited some of his English relatives, including florists in the Manning clan who had moved down to Dover, and found that Dover was a poor place to have a greenhouse during the war.

And, of course, that's the clue to the mystery of this fellow Manning. The fellow's an Englishman. English character runs deep in people, and it still runs deep in E. C. Manning. Take away his hat. (You'll have trouble doing it because he hates to give up a comfortable broken-in hat.) But take it anyway and give him a black Homburg. Then give him a longish black coat and hand him a tightly-furled black umbrella and send him stepping down Whitehall on his way to the House of Commons. There he is.

In thought and action, the fellow's an Englishman. In his appearance – and even more in his disappearance to the sanctuary of his castle on the river – the fellow's an Englishman. This may come as a surprise even to Ernest C. Manning, but it's the secret of his personality – a personality so baffling because it's so uncomplicated.

ABOUT THE AUTHOR
TONY CASHMAN

The author of this biography, Tony Cashman, went on to receive the Alberta Order of Excellence in 2014. It was the latest in a long line of awards including 'Edmontonian of the Century' in 2004, the Historical Society of Alberta annual award in 2010, and having a new Edmonton neighborhood named after him in 2011. Now at the age of 98, Mr. Cashman lives in Edmonton and continues writing stories about Alberta's history. His beloved wife, Veva, passed away in 2004. A large park was dedicated to him in June, 2021. He attended the ceremony and gave a speech, waving to the crowd.

The above picture is of Mr. Cashman in 1956, near the time of his writing this biographical sketch.

Tony Cashman was born in 1923 in Edmonton and went on to serve in the Canadian Air Force during WW II as a navigator on a Halifax bomber completing 30 missions over continental Europe. Some of his stories are recorded on the internet and available for the interested reader to look up.

After the war he attended Notre Dame University and returned to Edmonton to conduct his career as a journalist, author and broadcaster. He was noted for building a rapport with people, winning their confidence so they would share their life stories. No doubt this quality of Mr. Cashman's character played a large part in the Biographical Sketch he made of Premier Manning in 1958. Mr. Manning trusted him to produce a fair and honest description of his life. Mr. Cashman desired to bring history to life and he did that with E. C. Manning, at a time when the Premier was so little known except in the public arena. By preserving the Premier's story, the reader can better appreciate the vibrant history of Alberta during the Manning years, and know the man who helped make it happen. He brought Mr. Manning to life in this short booklet and with a touch of humor – helping the people of Alberta to know their Premier up-front and personal – making him real, transparent and human.

Tony Cashman retired in 1983 and went on to continue authoring books and eventually to writing plays about history. He had a profound belief in making history 'come to life,' in his plays and books. He has published more than sixteen books and ten plays, bringing to life many aspects of Edmonton's and Alberta's history. He has more than 700 pieces for his Edmonton Stories series alone. He truly deserves the accolades given him by the people of Edmonton and Alberta. We are fortunate that it was he who wrote the first biography on E. C. Manning because he knew the Premier in person and witnessed his leadership in the Alberta Legislature for years.

ADDENDUM 1
ERNEST C. MANNING'S SALVATION TESTIMONY
RADIO ADDRESS
CHICAGO, APRIL 9, 1948

The Hon. E. C. Manning was a guest speaker at the "America for Christ" rally held recently in Chicago. His sermon was broadcast over WMBI and WDLM radio, and was reprinted in the May, 1948, Prophetic Voice booklet. The portion of his message below is his personal testimony of salvation in 1925 while a seventeen-year-old farm boy living near Rosetown, Saskatchewan. He was saved through the preaching of William Aberhart broadcasting over CFCN Radio, Calgary.

"Perhaps I should tell you briefly how it came about, that I became a lowly subject of His heavenly kingdom and a grateful ambassador for Him. Like millions of others, I knew many things about Jesus Christ before I knew Him personally. His name was a familiar name. In childhood I learned many stories of His wonderful works in the days when He lived among men. His Word was a familiar book. Like millions of others, I subscribed as a matter of course to the teachings and ethics of what is commonly referred to as the Christian way of life. As a matter of course, I often attended His house of worship and sang with those assembled there,

> When I survey the wondrous cross
> On which the Prince of glory died,
> My richest gain I count but loss,
> And pour contempt on all my pride.

But one day I turned on my radio, just as you did this morning and from a distant city I heard a faithful ambassador of Jesus Christ bearing witness for his Lord. As I listened on that far off Sunday afternoon, I realized for the first time that there is an all – important difference between knowing about Jesus Christ and knowing Jesus Christ personally. It is one thing to be able to say I know about the Man of Galilee, I know about His miraculous birth, His marvelous life among men, His substitutionary death on the Cross of Calvary and His bodily resurrection from the dead. But it is something altogether different to meet Him personally as the Savior who died for you, and bow in His living presence a lost and helpless sinner to receive from Him forgiveness of sins, the gift of eternal life, and a new nature born of God. Then, and not until then, can you rise from your knees and say in truth and with joy,

> "Tis done, the great transaction's done,
> I am my Lord's and He is mine."

> *"For I know whom I have believed, and am persuaded that he is able to keep that which I have committed unto him against that day."* (2 Timothy 1:12)

That was my personal experience now over twenty years ago. The intervening years have been eventful and filled with many interesting experiences. Each passing year and each new experience has strengthened my conviction that mankind's greatest need is not more formal religion, not new creeds and dogmas, not better codes of social and moral ethics, but the greatest and most urgent need of every man and woman today is to know Jesus Christ personally as a real, living, divine Savior and Lord and coming King.

That's why this morning I want to talk to you, not about myself, but about Him, not about my opinions and beliefs, but about His blessed and perfect Will as recorded in the world's one and only infallible Book, the verbally inspired and divinely preserved Word of the living God."

ADDENDUM 2

THE HON. ERNEST C. MANNING'S LIFE AFTER 1958

"By and large, no provincial leader has ever earned and won more public respect, confidence and admiration than has been sustained over a remarkably long period by Premier Manning."
(Brian Brennan, Calgary Herald Tribute, February 21, 1996)

E. C. Manning continued as Premier of Alberta until 1968 when he retired from provincial politics. He could have continued but considered that the people and the Lord would decide when he should step aside. He wisely decided to leave the Premier's position at the peak of his success, leaving a legacy unequalled by any leader since. Brian Brennan details Premier Manning's achievements, including the last ten years as Premier and the time up until his going home to be with his Lord and Savior in 1996.

He was willing to enter federal politics in the late 1960s but the door did not open for him to do so. Canadians were enamored with Pierre Trudeau and had selected the left-leaning Robert Stanfield to become leader of the Progressive Conservative Party. Prime Minister Trudeau appointed Mr. Manning to the Canadian Senate in 1970, and there he remained until the age of mandatory retirement at 75 in 1983. Pierre Trudeau told E. C. Manning that he would rather have him in the Senate than out on the street talking to people. He recognized the impact that this Christian leader could have if he was given free rein to do so. Mr. Manning tried to have an impact in the Senate but could do little in a partisan body controlled by the Eastern elite establishment. He thought the Senate resembled a peaceful country graveyard.

All the while he served in the political world Mr. Manning continued to preach the Gospel of Jesus Christ on Canada's National Back to the Bible Hour. His radio messages can still be heard there on the first Sunday of every month on Global Outreach Missions. That is remarkable since he first began preaching on the radio with William Aberhart in 1930.

E. C. Manning's vision for Canada was a return to the Bible and Jesus Christ, with personal salvation being the bedrock decision of every person's life. Every one of his Bible messages end with an invitation to the listener to accept Jesus Christ as their personal Lord and Savior, as he did under William Aberhart's preaching on the radio in 1925.

He and his wife, Muriel, retired to Arizona in the late 1980s and enjoyed quiet years together out of the mainstream of public life. In 1996, at the age of 87, E. C. Manning passed away in Calgary, his beloved city. Many people paid their last respects to this great leader at his public funeral at the Jubilee Auditorium. Mr. Brennan's quote above is a tribute taken from that event.

Mr. Manning left a legacy of leadership that is hard to find today. In reviewing the performance of our Federal and Provincial leaders over the years it is becoming increasingly apparent that compromise and political correctness have taken center stage. There seems to be a lack of integrity and character in politics and society in general as our country drifts more and more toward the political left. Even the Conservatives are being dragged along by this trend that is being dictated mainly by the Liberal Party of Canada and Justin Trudeau – who is merely carrying out his own father's legacy of authoritarian leadership demonstrated between 1968 and 1984.

It may be time to look outside of mainstream academia for our future leaders. The university is producing most of today's leaders and that seems to be the problem. If the source is corrupted, so is the product. Manning was a farm boy who heard the Gospel and got saved at an early age. He had great capabilities but he was not molded by an anti-Christian academia, but by the teaching in William Aberhart's Bible Institute. He developed a strong Christian character and integrity which he maintained in politics and for the remainder of his life. Perhaps, just perhaps, this is what our country needs today in the political realm. If something does not change soon we are going to end up in a full-fledged dictatorship – and then it will be too late to change anything.

> *"For the transgression of a land many are the princes thereof: but by a man of understanding and knowledge the state thereof shall be prolonged."* (Proverbs 28:2)

www.ingramcontent.com/pod-product-compliance
Lightning Source LLC
Chambersburg PA
CBHW051048030426
42339CB00006B/245